ROSCOE PHOENIX

*Searching for a Forever Family
and a Warm Home*

by
Alina Paez

Copyright © 2023 by Alina Paez

All rights reserved.

No part of this book may be reproduced in any form or by any electronic or mechanical means, including information storage and retrieval systems, without written permission from the author, except for the use of brief quotations in a book review.

Published in the United States by:
Brillante Books LLC
office@brillantebooks.com

ISBN:

Ebook: 978-1-7377796-3-6
Paperback: 978-1-7377796-4-3
Hardcover: 978-1-7377796-5-0

*To all parents and caregivers who share their loving time
and help their loyal friend in sickness and good health.*

One who loves animals extends joy and compassion with a deeper understanding toward others of their own species.

Contents

Chapter One
My First Home 1

Chapter Two
The Sanctuary.................................... 5

Chapter Three
Meeting Roscoe 9

Chapter Four
Home Sweet Home 19

Chapter Five
Welcome Home Brother 27

Chapter Six
Seasons of Doggie Life........................... 33

Chapter Seven
Unexpected News 39

Chapter Eight
For the Sake of Love 43

Chapter Nine
Circle of Love................................... 47

Deep Love..51

Message from the Author 53

CHAPTER ONE

My First Home

"I am lost! Where is everybody? Hey! Drive carefully, walk on the sidewalks and follow the rules! Can you see the stop sign?" If my dear friend, Roscoe (aka *The Gladiator*), could be a human, he would say it loudly (but politely). If only he could speak, then his journey may have had a different ending. This is the story of Roscoe Phoenix, a beautiful boston terrier, from Virginia. A smart, funny, inquisitive, short but sturdy little dog.

One day, he ran away from his litter and wandered around the quiet roads of an unknown small town. He was extremely excited, exploring on his own, still carrying his little blanket with his teeth, walking with no direction at all. Suddenly, he started searching for his brothers and sisters, frantically looking all around, but found himself alone. He tried to find his way back to his litter, but it was late and too dark to see. Roscoe was lost but continued walking anyway. He was determined to find a place to stay warm, and he sure did! He stopped by a well-lit house with a cozy front porch and settled in for the night.

Early the following day, Ms. Love, the owner of the house, was ready to take her bloodhound, Bo, for a long walk. As soon as she opened her door, she saw Roscoe sleeping with a blanket on her front porch! She was in awe, seeing him as a gift she would want to care for and treasure forever. Loyal Bo was standing next to her and making unusual sounds while smelling Roscoe. She reassured him gently, saying, "Bo, this is our new friend, say no more." They were both gazing upon him curiously when Roscoe woke with a start. He noticed the two onlookers and then immediately grabbed his blanket and started biting it anxiously, not knowing what would happen to him next. Ms. Love said, "What a surprise! Someone left us a precious puppy! I love his marks, his size, and the way he snores. He is such a cutie pie! He has arrived at our home for a reason!" Bo gave her a strange look and went back into the house towards the fireplace, where he jumped into his big old bed, and covered his eyes with his long floppy ears.

Meanwhile, Ms. Love picked Roscoe up, took him inside, fed him, and bathed him. Roscoe let his little old blanket go and played with her enthusiastically, licking her rosy cheeks countless times. Then, he ran all over the house and found Bo, who welcomed the exciting moment and shared his favorite toy, inviting Roscoe to play tug-o-war! Roscoe showed his strength and finally, Bo laid down, exhausted from having too much fun. Then, the little black and white terrier ran back toward Ms. Love and gave her a sweet look, like he was asking her to give him a new family and a warm home to snooze in! "Take me in and love me. I promise I will be good, and I will always love you!" he spoke with a soft crying noise.

He stole her heart immediately. Roscoe was loved and well taken care of by his new family. He had a new momma, a warm home, food, and a new big brother called Bo.

CHAPTER TWO

The Sanctuary

All was great until one unexpected day when his Momma got sick and could not take care of Roscoe anymore. By then, he had become a well-trained, smart, three-year-old friendly family member with all the positive qualities a well-mannered dog should have. But the decision had already been made. Roscoe would be separated from his family for the second time, no matter how polite or friendly he was. His new home would be "The Boston Terrier Sanctuary" in East Tennessee, a place where older dogs would spend the rest of their lives receiving extra care and love. The sanctuary accepted Ms. Love's request to relinquish Roscoe due to her suddenly deteriorated health. They agreed to welcome Roscoe in the first week of December. On that fateful day, Ms. Love woke up early in the morning, had breakfast, fed Roscoe and Bo, and took them for a short walk. She stopped in a park and took a picture of the two boys together. Then, she put the brothers in the back of her car and started driving to Roscoe's soon-to-be new home. It was a quiet ride. It was like both pets would sense the sadness in the air. It was their last ride together as a family.

The raindrops began to fall when they arrived. Ms. Love stayed in the car for a few minutes. She did not want to let him go but knew that he would be better cared for by his friendly new caregivers. When she finally got out of the car and approached the building, someone from the sanctuary opened the door and provided help with the paperwork.

Roscoe was warmly welcomed by the staff and several (much older) boston terriers. His presence was a refreshing reminder of the glorious youthful times these senior dogs once had, bringing them back some hope to keep having fun just like they had in their good old days. With the excitement of making new friends, Roscoe felt distracted for a moment. When the other dogs settled down and left him to settle in, Roscoe sat still; he did not know what to do in this unfamiliar environment. He started shaking a little bit. He knew something strange was going to happen. Finally, the hardest moment arrived. The family had to say their good-byes. They had to detach from love and family and take different, unknown routes. To Roscoe, this all felt so wrong. He became confused and tried to run back to the car, but Ms. Love reluctantly picked him up and took him back to the sanctuary door.

Roscoe did not understand what was going on, he was starting to panic. He kept licking the tears falling from Ms. Love's rosy cheeks. This was not the usual way to go for a walk, no, not at all! If he could, he would be talking again in his language of love and say: "It is ok mommy. Please do not cry, take me with you and I will be good to you!" But it did not work. Again, he felt sad and alone. Ms. Love left the room and before Roscoe knew it, she was gone. Bo had been waiting in the car, sadly howling goodbyes to his little brother. Roscoe stared out the window as those howls faded away and, instead of his family, he was left with his old blanket and his favorite animal toy. He cuddled the blanket and started chewing on it, which he did for a long time until he finally fell asleep.

That night, Roscoe dreamed of sitting by the warm fireplace next to Bo. He tried not to feel like he had lost another battle - the painful battle of losing his dear family. Waking through the night, Roscoe cuddled his blanket and toy closer to him, trying to hold onto the fond memories of his family, while dreaming again of finding a forever home.

Roscoe never gave up. He was a survivor, with lots of unique qualities in his favor. He was short but muscular and strong. He displayed a tenacious attitude while keeping a friendly and soft disposition toward other canines and human acquaintances. His sensitive and inquisitive nature would allow him to have a good relationship with other members of his new pack and be liked by all. Roscoe won the trust of the other dogs and became the leader of the senior pack while he was only a young adult dog. And there was more to discover about him. Sometimes, it felt like Roscoe could communicate with humans through his beautiful eyes and body language. He would look at his bowl, look back at them, and bark at a human to ask for food. He would stand by the back door and politely bark until someone arrived to open the door so the dogs could go outside to play or use the bathroom. He would come to a human or another dog holding his favorite toy to play tag-o-war. He would even nod his head to the left or right to ask "what is going on?" If you were paying attention, Roscoe could talk to you, embrace you, and love you.

As the days passed, Roscoe realized he had a new caregiver mom, more friends, food, toys, and a cozy warm place to live in again. He was now part of the Boston Terrier Sanctuary family. Roscoe tried his best to be happy. He and his new friends were invincible. He knew he needed to help himself and others to survive in this world. He already knew how to follow the rules to find his forever home. His new foster mom at the sanctuary noticed his talents among all the other dogs. He was an obedient dog with a special, radiant look that earned him a new nickname. A week later he was officially named "Roscoe Phoenix." He was usually looking up at someone's eyes, birds, butterflies, the sky, or the moon. Sometimes, it seemed like he was talking to the stars. His fur would shine in the dark and seem to compete with the brightness of the sun.

Roscoe Phoenix had a new life. As a young new leader, he and his senior pack earned the nickname "The Gladiators." The Gladiators were warriors, trying to survive the unexpected and overcome a defiant reality as a small pack in a big world, while still never giving up the hope of finding their forever homes.

CHAPTER THREE

Meeting Roscoe

Elaine was reluctantly browsing for a new pet. Although she refused to admit it, she kept pondering whether she could ever think about getting another dog again. Her dilemma was whether or not she could open her heart and welcome a new pet experience, which would include extra commitments into her daily routines. Or should she just find another enjoyable activity that would not disrupt her current busy lifestyle?

Halloween was around the corner; a bunch of tasks and to-do lists from both home and work were falling like leaves from sturdy tree branches and piling up in all directions. Elaine tried to collect them, solve them, and send them away diligently by utilizing her own set of tools – tools charged up with time organization, constant effort, and a positive attitude. Still, regardless of the intensity of activities and meaningful moments, she thought it might not hurt to keep looking for another four-legged friendly pooch that would love to have a new family and a warm home. She gradually realized that getting a new, lovable, and loyal companion was the right choice, especially at this time of the year. She understood that she was not replacing her previous boston terrier, who had passed away a few months ago. As days passed, there was a refreshing sense of certainty in the air, removing any clouds of doubt. Elaine was prepared to open her heart and make her wishes come true.

She sat in front of her computer and began searching intensively for a boston terrier to rescue and make her companion. She stopped at an unusual site. It was a sanctuary site that allows senior dogs to have shelter, food, and a place they can call home. The site contained a message related to a much younger dog that had arrived a few weeks ago and was in desperate need of a forever home. He was only three years old and his posting introduced him as Roscoe Phoenix. There was a message below his pictures that described his past and present journey.

The listing looked like this:

Roscoe Phoenix VA
Boston Terrior

Hi,

My name is Roscoe. I am three years old. I am neutered, house trained, and have lots of energy to share with all! I am friendly with people and other dogs. I like to play with toys, hold my blanket tight, and do some cuddling too!

In case you're wondering how I ended up being at the Sanctuary I got lost almost three years ago. A sweet lady found me, adopted me, and loved me until she got sick and could not take care of me anymore. She helped me grow up playful and strong. I miss her a lot, but I am moving forward with this note.

If you are into fashion, I am too! I have a natural tuxedo, I love rain jackets, sport tshirts, and other accessories. They make me look elegant and smooth. I am in to sweaters, although they can change my body temperature and maybe my mood.

My second name is Phoenix because I look at the stars and other living things meaningfully. I hope I can look up to my new owner sometime soon! I am in search of someone who can take care of me and give me a forever home. In return, I will fill your heart with lots of love! If you think I am the best match for you, please give us a call. If not, look at my other friends and give them a chance to spread the joy!

Sincerely,

Roscoe Phoenix
The Boston Terrier Sanctuary
www.insearchofaforeverhome.org
615.123.4567

The listing solidified Elaine's decision to pursue Roscoe's adoption. She replied to the message and expressed her interest in him. Almost immediately, Elaine got a message that strengthened her hopes. Here is the list of questions she asked and the answers she got.

1. Is Roscoe still available? Yes
2. Is Roscoe a boston terrier? Yes
3. Is Roscoe a trained dog? Yes
4. Is Roscoe an obedient dog? Yes
5. Is Roscoe a healthy dog? Yes
6. Is Roscoe playful? Yes
7. Does Roscoe interact well with other dogs? Yes!
8. Does Roscoe like to go for walks? Yes
9. Does Roscoe want to have a new family and a warm home? Yes
10. Is Roscoe a rescue dog? He is a surrendered dog. He previously lived in a lovable home and although he is too young to live in a sanctuary, he is like family to us. He is not a rescued dog; he has rescued us!

After discussing the pros and cons of adoption with her husband, Mike, and taking the time to reflect on it, the decision was made. Mike was willing to help Elaine all the way through. It was their first time adopting a dog from a sanctuary. The answer to her first question was all they needed to know. By now, it did not matter whether Roscoe was healthy, smart, playful, or not; they would have taken him home just as he was. Elaine needed Roscoe as much as he needed her. Still, she wondered if she would be the best match for him. She also thought about the impact of her personality and schedules on his overall quality of life. She was ready to adapt and willing to change her lifestyle and daily routines in return for happy and exciting moments with her soon-to-be companion.

Naturally, Elaine worried about leaving him alone during the day although her reasoning did comfort her, knowing that at least she was providing him with a warm place he would call home. Elaine was extremely thoughtful; she would try to put herself in Roscoe's place and imagine questions he might have asked if only he could talk, such as:

1. Is my new home near the sanctuary?
2. Can I visit my friends now and then?
3. Is there anyone at home during the day?
4. How often do I get cuddles?

5. Do I get to eat a lot?

6. Will I have a chance to travel and explore new places?

7. Are there any other dogs or cats at home?

8. Will I get dressed like a fancy dog?

9. Will I walk at least twice a day?

10. Will I sleep in a kennel or your bed?

She knew that their expectations would be synchronized. Both needed each other's companionship and love. Elaine and her family were ready to welcome Roscoe and include him as a family member by providing him with a warm home with unconditional love.

Elaine returned to her computer desk, sat in front of her computer, and looked at the site one more time. There he was in front of her. It was a picture of Roscoe Phoenix biting his blanket and sending love. She looked at the second picture and there he was again. Roscoe was posing for the picture like he knew this was his only chance to find a loving home. After getting more information about the organization, Elaine completed an application and talked to Marlene, Roscoe's caregiver, over the phone. A couple of months later, Elaine's application was finally approved.

The night before Elaine met Roscoe was December 23rd. Roscoe Phoenix had to relinquish his "Leader of the Gladiators" title and say "adios" to his faithful pack. They all wished they could find a place they could call "home" too but they were overjoyed for Roscoe. But still, they knew their vibrant leader was going away. They were looking at each other sadly as if part of their youth was leaving them. If their howling and barking could have been translated into words, they might have said, "Lucky you! We will miss you, but we know we will see the same stars. Remember us when you play outside. Listen to the birds singing, see the butterflies dancing during the day and watch the moon at night. They will remind you of us and how we all stick together as a pack day and night anywhere in the world. We will always be your gladiator family, no matter where you go."

On his last night at The Boston Terrier Sanctuary, Roscoe could not sleep. He was restless. He tried to find comfort in biting his little blanket and cuddling it closely. Eventually, Roscoe fell asleep.

The exciting day finally arrived. Elaine and Mike were ready for their journey early that morning. They traveled east across the Tennessee plateau from Brentwood (a suburb south of Nashville) to Maryville (a town in the foothills of the Blue Ridge Mountains). Both were determined to bring Roscoe to his new home on Christmas Eve. Simultaneously, Marlene was driving Roscoe from Bristol, Virginia to Maryville, where they would meet his new family.

Once all parties arrived in Maryville, they met in a pet store parking lot. Elaine recognized the black car Marlene had described to her in an email as it pulled into the parking lot. Elaine and Mike felt anxious as they watched the car come to a stop approximately thirty feet in front of them. Through the windows, they could see a dog sticking his head up with pointy ears twitching anxiously. It was Roscoe. He was wearing a Santa outfit.

Elaine and Mike reacted quickly and ran toward the car. Marlene gave Roscoe a goodbye kiss while still holding him and then put him in Mike's arms. Roscoe was embraced and carried to his new mom Elaine, who welcomed him with gratefulness and an open heart. At that moment, everyone's anxieties faded away. They had an instant connection. Roscoe was part of a family again and that day, he knew he was going home.

CHAPTER FOUR

Home Sweet Home

Roscoe arrived at his new home early in the evening of December 24th. He was immediately taken to the backyard where he walked around the entire fence, marking his playground area with his scent to let other animals in the area know that this was his home. Then, he turned around and walked toward his human family. Mike opened the back door and Roscoe entered his new home for the first time.

Welcoming a new family member during the holiday season added a special, magical feeling to the moment. It was soon confirmed for Elaine that she and Roscoe were a perfect match for each other. They had many things in common and were eager to begin their new fun life together. Elaine had even compiled a list of things they would do together:

- walk together
- listen to the birds singing
- go shopping

- smell food flavors
- travel and explore new places
- cuddle and stay warm

But all anxieties and wonderings about the past and future were overshadowed by living in the present and enjoying the simplicity of life. They both wanted to create a magical match, a forever bond, all while making new friends along the way.

At the beginning of January, the family was trying to adapt to their new routines. Mike was absorbed with his job but always made himself available to join his wife and Roscoe to go for long walks, especially on weekends. Elaine returned to her job as a teacher after the holiday break and realized that Roscoe needed more attention during the day while she and Mike were gone; he needed a new pet sitter. But first, she wanted to make sure Roscoe was fully trained and prepared to welcome Regina, the pet sitter Elaine had previously worked with. Even though the sanctuary said Roscoe had been trained, he attended obedience school again. He quickly graduated and earned two certificates for passing the most rigorous obedience exams.

Elaine contacted Regina a few weeks later and asked if she would be available to take care of Roscoe. Elaine already trusted her because she took excellent care of her previous boston terrier and loved her job. They set a time to meet and decide if she and Roscoe would be a good match as well. Regina came over the following day. As soon as she met Roscoe, he gave her his irresistible look, and then, there was a moment of silence, only broken when Regina laughed and said: "He is so cute and so well-trained!"

The meeting went so well that Regina did not hesitate to take care of Roscoe. She agreed to visit him each afternoon, walk him for fifteen to twenty minutes, play with him, then make sure he had enough food and water to last until Elaine and Mike returned in the evening. Regina always honored her word; she walked Roscoe and treated him tenderly, and Roscoe was always happy to see her. Regina would write short notes about each of Roscoe's main events of the day. Below, you will see a few notes that she shared in his daily journal:

01/11

Roscoe was a real trooper today. Back for a treat and fresh water.

02/04

Lots of sniffing and investigating at each tree along the way. Treat and fresh water.

Monday, 11:45

Roscoe enjoyed sniffing and scratching at the ground. He can really pick up some dirt!

Went potty and had a BM. Back in for his first treat and a drink. 🙂

—Regina

10/24

A great visit. Roscoe was full of his usual energy and curiosity. He went potty and had a BM. Had some water and a treat.

Two years later, Roscoe had bloomed into a very elegant and polite boston terrier, as well as a beloved companion. By then, he was five years old. Below you will see a few more notes that will give you a better understanding of Roscoe's personality:

Friday, 1/6 11:15 am

Roscoe was asleep when I got here. He looked so cute all snuggled into his blankets.

We had a nice walk. He went potty and had a BM. Back for his snack and fresh water.

05/25

Roscoe got petted by ten people who were walking in the neighborhood. He was very polite.

Happy summer. Will miss my little friend 🙂

—Regina

Elaine's teaching time was ending and a family vacation was already planned for the following week. Mike and Elaine were looking forward to enjoying walking on the beach, exploring new places, and having a pleasant time while being away from their usual responsibilities and schedules. And Roscoe was included in the family vacation! He truly was part of the family pack! A few days later, they departed for South Carolina. Roscoe's first out-of-state vacation was a visit to Myrtle Beach. He had a fantastic time! He was inquisitive with new smells, sounds of birds singing, and the ocean breeze while comfortably strolling early in the mornings and late in the evenings when the weather was not too hot or humid. Roscoe even took the time to pose elegantly for pictures when asked.

While enjoying the pleasant weather and nice walks along the beach, Elaine was also thinking how nice it would be to walk Roscoe with a new buddy, maybe even one of his gladiator friends.

CHAPTER FIVE

Welcome Home Brother

Elaine and Mike agreed on the idea of adding a new pet to their family. They both felt that Roscoe would be greatly benefitted from the ability to interact and play with another dog, and it would equally benefit another dog from the sanctuary.

By the first weekend of July, they had contacted The Boston Terrier Sanctuary and were happy to learn there was a dog that their caretakers thought would be a good fit for their family. This dog's name was Buster, he was four years old, and had been at the sanctuary for almost a year. Although Roscoe and Buster's paths did not overlap at the sanctuary, they already had a few things in common: they both arrived at the sanctuary at age three, were part of the gladiators' pack, had a history of living with families, and they both wanted a chance to find a forever family.

The following week, the whole family visited the sanctuary to meet Buster. Roscoe had a chance to interact with Buster and they seemed to get along fine while going for a short walk along a grassy path. A week later, the family welcomed Buster into their home.

At first, Roscoe felt strange. He did not want to play with Buster or interact with him at all. He stood still for a while, looking in another direction and not towards Buster. He did not like the idea of having another "gladiator" in his home. He was in shock that there was another dog in his house. Roscoe and Buster were completely different. Roscoe loved going on short walks, Buster could keep walking for miles. Roscoe would only eat food from his bowl, while his brother would anxiously eat food from any bowl. Roscoe wanted to play with his toy quietly, while the new family member wildly explored many toys at once. Roscoe loved to sleep quietly in his private tent. Buster would make loud noises while dreaming, wake up, and end up sleeping comfortably on the sofa.

Sometimes Roscoe would give Elaine his wondering looks by twisting his neck to the side, back and forth, as if asking questions about Buster in his way. "What is going on? I cannot believe it! Did you take him to training school? You'll have to work on his manners! How can I help?" Buster did eventually attend and graduate from obedience school. But vacation time was over, and the family had learned that the adoption process was going to take longer than they originally expected.

During that time, Roscoe looked indifferent. He isolated himself in his tent, chewing his favorite toy for longer periods. He even lost his appetite for a while. Elaine and Mike reassured him in so many ways that their love for him would last forever. But Roscoe's uncertainties were displayed through his indifferent attitude. Roscoe's ability to accept Buster was even more challenged when Buster would not recognize his gladiator leadership status. It did not take long for Roscoe to realize it was time to "share" his home rather than lead Buster. It was not an easy task for Roscoe to accept him as part of his new pack but his love and trust in Elaine and Mike as his forever family gave him more comfort. He was not going to be replaced but instead, he was going to have a new brother to play with.

Soon enough, the whole family understood their differences. They realized that just because they had come from the same rescue home, did not mean the two dogs would behave comparably. Accepting their differences, focusing on their strengths, helping them to overcome their challenges, and learning to get along with each other while following household rules were as important as providing shelter and food. All of them would need to prove their successes later when interacting with others outside of their family environment.

Elaine hoped Regina would not run away from the new additional job and, proving herself as the incredible caregiver they knew her to be, she did not. Regina looked at the new family member and knew it would be more difficult, but agreed to give it a try. She reinforced rules while caring for both brothers and helping them to compromise for each other. For example, Roscoe would have to walk a little longer while Buster would need to go on shorter walks. In the end, both would walk an average of three times a day.

Eventually, time worked in their favor. Roscoe and Buster became better adjusted by learning their new routines for eating, playing, and walking next to each other, synchronizing their pace to perfection. The recipe for love had some basic ingredients of patience, perseverance, hope (especially on stormy days), and of compromise. The sweetness and saltiness of combined experiences strengthened their bond over time and helped them recognize a taste of delicious, unforgettable moments with a forever family and a warm home.

By Labor Day weekend, they had all become adjusted to their new routines. The two gladiators were grateful for sunny days, singing birds, butterflies everywhere, and a cozy place to stay.

CHAPTER SIX

Seasons of Doggie Life

Roscoe had a full schedule during summertime. His first activity was going for a long walk early in the morning to avoid the strong upcoming heat of the day. Unusual sunny, breezy summer days would allow him to run for a little bit while enjoying the freshness of the air. This was the season in which Roscoe would prefer to walk on shady trails and paths surrounded by peaceful lakes with beautiful geese and swans on his side. He would stop by trees and smell them for a while but not before leaving his unique marks! Another important assignment he had was to walk around the grill when Elaine and Mike barbecued outside. He loved his summer job and the smell of delicious grilled meats and vegetables.

Roscoe's summer routine was complemented by one more assignment, which was to look through the window at birds and butterflies flying around the garden areas on a hot, humid afternoon.

His last summer assignment before going for an evening walk would be gardening with Elaine. Roscoe would sit outside on the patio chair, looking at the backyard while Elaine planted seeds, bulbs, and other ornamental flowering plants during springtime. He would patiently wait for his beloved human mom until she was done gardening. Sometimes, Elaine was reminded about the extraordinary length of time gardening would take while others were waiting for her. Then, Roscoe would walk around the garden to let her know it was time to stop and move on.

Another season soon arrived, and the family would welcome fall while saying goodbye to the annuals, butterflies, and colorful singing birds flying up high. Roscoe knew the wind would be on his side, allowing him to enjoy the breeze of warmer summer memories while going for long walks or to a pumpkin patch. The fall season would end with a special gathering time: The Annual Boston Terrier Event where Roscoe and Buster could see, sniff, and play with their other four-legged boston terrier peers. Who knows if they would be able to see them again? It was their time to fully enjoy the remains of nice weather and walk along the colorful leaves of the fall.

Halloween preparation was challenging for Roscoe and his new brother. Elaine and Mike tried to be careful that neither chocolate nor candy were allowed near their favorite companions. They feared that the events and excitement of the holiday would overlook their pet's needs.

Winter brought many changes for the family. The hustle and bustle of the upcoming holiday time affected Roscoe's senses and well-being tremendously. He started eating more food and drinking water excessively. He tried to do his best in all circumstances but Roscoe did not enjoy the chilly weather. He would never let go of his blanket; he would come into the house, stop by his bed, get his blanket, and carry it with his teeth up the stairs into his favorite room (the family room). This was Roscoe's favorite room because this is where his family most often gathered all together, giving him the perfect opportunity to be the center of attention by playing around cutely. He gave his audience plenty of entertainment; showing his strength with a tug-o-war game, giving lots of licks, and receiving lots of belly rubs in return. But other than these playful bouts indoors, Roscoe usually slept much more during the colder time of year.

As soon as the winter began to fade, the family would start going for peaceful walks on short trails again. The whole family basked in the sun on those early spring days. It seemed to say, "warmer days are ahead," and fueled them all with hope. Sometimes, Elaine, Roscoe, and Buster would stop all at once and notice little yellow flowers blooming quietly on the side of a trail or see a graceful dear crossing their paths. It was wonderful when they rediscovered the unique interaction with other living things such as plants, trees, mammals, birds, and insects. Spring reminds us in such a tender way of the harmony in coexistence between all things in the world.

Each season would bring Roscoe a new routine and some new friends. Roscoe was very skilled in finding different things to love about all the seasons of life. He learned quickly that all seasons would fade and then come back again. He knew how to embrace each timeframe to the fullest and was grateful that no matter what, he already had found a forever warm home surrounded with quiet graceful notes of love.

CHAPTER SEVEN

Unexpected News

The following Christmas Eve, something strange happened. Roscoe's right eye did not move at all. Elaine took him to the ophthalmology veterinarian and discovered that half of his face was paralyzed. Elaine also noticed he was drinking an excessive amount of water during the day. She decided to take him to the emergency veterinary hospital immediately. It was soon after the family learned that Roscoe had Cushing's Disease. The veterinarian on call explained to Elaine that Roscoe would live approximately two and a half years but that he may seem fine for now.

The shocking news had Elaine trembling while taking Roscoe back to the car. It was difficult for her to accept that Roscoe had any kind of disease at his age; he was only seven and a half years old. She needed to share Roscoe's new health condition with Mike. She went straight home, put Roscoe into his bed, and directed herself to her computer. Then, she started gathering as much information about this disease as she could. The facts were in front of her, on her screen—Roscoe's chances of recovering from this painful illness were extremely low. Elaine shared the unexpected news with Mike as soon as he arrived from work.

They made an appointment to visit Roscoe's primary veterinarian to discuss the diagnosis and how best to move forward. The veterinarian's advice was to provide medication to make Roscoe feel better, although they were reminded that there would be a time when his medication would stop working on his little body. But there was nothing they wouldn't do for Roscoe, so Mike and Elaine prepared to adjust their daily home activities, taking into consideration Roscoe's new health condition.

Sometimes good moments end sooner than expected. A cloud of uncertainties and fear became visible on the family's horizon. Roscoe's medication made him feel better for a while and the family tried to make each day a special one. They continued taking Roscoe to parks and some doggie events on his good days, but would rather keep him at home on hot or rainy days. As time passed, new routines evolved into more special, meaningful moments to remember. One of their favorite routines was taking turns cuddling with him on the couch and feeling his little heart beating while embracing him. Resting together was especially enjoyed at the end of a long working day. Though this time was difficult, it was also a reminder of their precious family and the time they had together to enjoy the little things. Elaine spent a lot of time researching and learning more about alternative treatments to help Roscoe. She wished to be in a different world. She would fall asleep and dream that eternal, simple, wonderful days would never go away.

Two years later, Roscoe became more fragile. The sickness started showing its more devastating effects on him. Roscoe the Gladiator was a warrior, defending his own life and well-being since puppyhood. But it was different this time. He was fighting against an invisible enemy that carried heavy destructive weapons that targeted his whole body. The family was walking on unknown trails with broken hearts under stormy, tearful days that would erase all paths of hope for recovery. It was difficult to accept that Roscoe's destiny was already posted on a calendar.

Roscoe's immune system was gradually becoming weaker and weaker. He lost weight, regardless of the amount of food he was given. He continued going for shorter and shorter walks. By the end of January of the following year, the disease was taking even more control of him. Their dear gladiator was losing battle after battle and Elaine and Mike could only watch, helpless to ease Roscoe's suffering any more than they already had.

A couple of months later, Elaine, Mike, Roscoe, and Buster all traveled to New York. While there, Roscoe got sick and was immediately taken to the emergency veterinary hospital. He was able to recover from that particular bout of sickness and conquer a major battle. After seeing what a natural fighter Roscoe was, the veterinarian provided a new treatment they thought could help Roscoe. This set the family on a shining path of hope. The sun was falling upon them, warming their souls, and making them smile—at least for a while.

A few months later, on the morning of July 11th, Roscoe got extremely sick at home in Tennessee. Elaine took him to the nearest emergency clinic and stayed with him as long as she could. The following morning, she learned that Roscoe was not responding to the medications he was being given. The veterinarian decided to take him to the main hospital, they couldn't just give up. Elaine embraced Roscoe and kept him in her arms while Mike drove to the hospital. Tears came steadily from her face; her heart was in constant pain, but she knew he was still feeling their forever love. Roscoe was surrounded by familiar sounds, smells, and his family's love. He knew how much he was loved.

Roscoe passed away in Elaine's arms on their way to the hospital. At that moment, their lives changed forever. He was ten years old.

CHAPTER EIGHT

For the Sake of Love

Elaine and Mike changed routes from the hospital to the pet cremation center the veterinarian had already told them about. They carried Roscoe into the facility and were given time to say their goodbyes there. Then, the moment to acknowledge Roscoe as part of the past became a present reality. He was always going to be a part of their family and their life journey, but it was time to recognize he was out of this world and write a farewell message to him. At the entrance, there was a white memorial wall filled with hundreds of happy and sad written messages from families who had lost a pet. Messages to and about life moments that left intimate marks on people's hearts. These unforgettable, emotional messages reminded them that they were not alone or misunderstood in the love of their family dog.

In a quiet moment waiting in the cremation center, Elaine and Mike reflected on Roscoe's quiet bravery and perseverance. In a way, remembering Roscoe's endless strength gave them the strength to confront the sense of loss and to accept the fact that sometimes there are things that are out of their control. Elaine and Mike had prepared for the worst while still sharing all that is good and positive with others. They were able to transform their challenging emotional experience into resilience tools to protect themselves from despair and survive in this world.

Later, Elaine and Mike walked toward the wall and wrote their goodbye messages on it. They also found their previous messages written when they had lost their first two boston terriers. The first one was written a decade ago on March 11th, when they lost Little Debbie at the age of twelve and a half. The second one was written on August 10th, when they lost Rudy at the age of fifteen. They found a small place next to Rudy's message to write a goodbye message for Roscoe. Elaine took up the black marker and started writing her message to Roscoe, telling him he was very much loved and how grateful they were for him, with tears streaming down her face the entire time. She continued writing and expressed her sadness for losing him, not because of old age, but because of a painful disease. She described how much she had tried to keep him healthier. Finally, she remembered giving Roscoe her best smile and happy praising commands while seeing her strong gladiator become more fragile day by day. Then, she stopped writing. Her message ended by saying: "You will always have a forever family and a warm home, in heaven and earth. Until the next time we meet, and you welcome me again." Mike's message was shorter. He wanted to complete the process and console Elaine as soon as possible. He reminded her that Buster, Roscoe's brother, was still waiting for them at home.

They left the memorial room carrying the pain and sadness of their loss in their hearts and minds. On their way home, Elaine could not stop thinking about things she could have done differently to save Roscoe's life. But she also reflected on moving forward; what that would look like and how they could do it. It did not mean forgetting Roscoe, but changing a sad outcome into a learning experience, especially when they did not have control over it. She thought about how humans had a choice to bond with a favorite pet, to share their love and loyalty at their own pace. Even in the darkest of moments, Elaine was grateful that these interactions became a rewarding relationship that supplied sweet memories and joy. Finally, Elaine noticed the heavy rain coming down. The car stopped on the driveway; Elaine and Mike arrived solemnly home.

CHAPTER NINE

Circle of Love

Elaine had kept a little folder for Roscoe from the age of three through the end of his life. It contained all his wellness information and details about his daily life, things she always wanted to remember. She also kept his original papers from his previous families describing what he went through since he was a little puppy. There was one more element Elaine needed to understand from Roscoe to get closure. As she closed the circle of love, she looked around in nature, trying to find something that would remind her of him. She soon discovered the loving interaction of all of Roscoe's friends: birds and butterflies, the rain, and even herself. As a human, Elaine was sometimes misled into believing she was on this painful path alone. But as she observed all the things in nature that Roscoe loved so deeply, she saw that the whole world (his whole world) could feel his loss right along with her. Elaine felt much less alone when she realized this.

On the day they lost Roscoe when they arrived home Elaine and Mike saw a group of small black birds flying toward the bottom edge of the roof. They were lining up, one next to the other all around the edge of the roof, surrounding their entire house. They sat there for at least two minutes, undisturbed by anything. It was as if they were acknowledging the pain and sadness of the moment and paying their respects to Roscoe, their special friend. They knew he would not be coming back home. It was an unforgettable moment for Elaine and Mike, in which nature expressed itself on this rainy day.

The rain stopped and the sunshine appeared a few minutes later. Elaine went out to the backyard and stood in one of Roscoe's favorite spots. She looked around tearfully, walking around her backyard and continuing her search for Roscoe's presence through nature. Suddenly, a beautiful and quite large white butterfly appeared and danced in front of Elaine delicately, exactly ten times. One time for each year of Roscoe's life. A feeling of hope appeared in her mind and she felt as if Roscoe was not saying goodbye forever. She was reminded of his love for birds, butterflies, and other living things. How grateful she was for the chance to receive his unconditional love and how grateful he was on earth, day by day, for the love and care he received from Elaine and Mike, his forever family.

Eventually, Elaine and Mike sold their home and moved away to the east coast. They took Roscoe's unconditional love and memories with them.

Elaine still enjoys walking with Buster. They do not go for long walks anymore, but shorter, slower walks that give them time to admire the splendor of each season. They appreciate all the trees, birds, and all living things they encountered and felt deeply connected to mother earth, or "Mama Pacha," as others would say. They have all grown a little older and continue treasuring their sweet memories and creating a path of love everywhere they go, hoping to arrive at an eternal destination with dignity, knowing they tried their best. Elaine has certainty that she and Roscoe's paths will cross again to reunite and walk together in search of their forever home.

Now and then, Elaine opens a hidden door covered with the vines of everyday rules, responsibilities, and obligations and enters a quiet, reflective room where she looks through the memory window and brings the unique events of each season to life. She has no regrets and does not look back. She grabs a few special moments, takes them with her, and stores them in her deep memory library. Her past events are eternally treasured in her heart and the lessons learned have served her well. Suddenly, she is distracted by the barking of her neighbor's dog. Elaine notices the present moment calling her again. Buster has waited patiently for her. She stops and says: "Time to go for a walk, my dear friend."

Deep Love

Walking through the path of loss
I find your picture and stop the clock
Happy memories become alive
Both of us racing together in perfect weather.
Passing through pleasant, glorious days.
Hearing the beautiful sound of singing birds
Water twinkling by the creek and the albino deer
steps searching for something to eat.
Sharing joyful times with others
to meet and greet.

While loving every living thing
Reality many times has taken us apart
We have also walked on rocky trails
we know life can be hard
your unconditional deep love
reminds me how precious you are

Responsive silence in the air
We have been searching for help
I can now recall my despair
No one can hear us,
We are alone on this uneven trail

Roscoe Phoenix

I hold this picture for a moment
It is time to put it aside. I cannot stay.
I can keep the happy moments and let
The sad ones go away.

Message from the Author

If by any chance you have a four-legged companion, allow them to fill your heart with their unconditional love and loyalty. Find happy moments in the simple things that nature offers and enjoy the long walks toward a better future.

Roscoe Phoenix

www.ingramcontent.com/pod-product-compliance
Lightning Source LLC
Chambersburg PA
CBHW040501110526
44587CB00032B/32